I AM H.E.R. (Healed.Empowered.Restored)

BURNED

But Not Broken

by

Tamara Knighten

with Sharon Rosario

My Scars, My Story

The Journey That Inspired My Confidence!

Burned But Not Broken

Dedication

This book is dedicated to my mother and sister, Sharon and Antoinette Rosario. You are my strength and my rock! Thank you for always being in my corner! I love you both!

Acknowledgements

First and foremost, I would like to thank God for being the head of my life. Without Him, I would be broken. He has taken my broken pieces and made a masterpiece and to Him I give all the Glory!

I would like to say thank you to my mother, Sharon Rosario, for loving me unconditionally and for the unwavering support you have given me throughout the years. Thank you so much for encouraging me to write this book. I could not have accomplished it without you!

Special thanks to my sister, Antoinette (Toni) Rosario. We have literally been through the fire, but I couldn't have picked a better person to be by my side. Through thick and thin you were always there! Thank you for being an awesome sister and friend! I love you to pieces!

To my father, Max Knighten, thank you for never looking at me with judging eyes. Thank you for allowing me to express myself however and whenever I needed to. I couldn't have gotten through this without your counsel and for that I am truly grateful. I'm so proud of you and appreciate you very much!

To my stepfather, Julio E. Rosario, thank you for loving me like your very own. You are heaven-sent and I love you so much!

To my brother Larry, you are, by far, one of the funniest people I know! You have a natural gift and talent that I can't wait for the whole world to see! Every time you come around, you give us a reason to laugh for hours, days and years thereafter. I also want to thank you for the gifts you have blessed us with named Sonja, my beautiful niece, Divinity and my handsome nephews, Kael and Jheckel. Eyes have not seen and ears have not heard the great things to come from this family! I can't wait to see it manifest! I love you all!

Burned But Not Broken

To my niece, Kayla Bowman, I write because of you. You are truly my daily inspiration. Every time I hear that you're writing, it makes me write more. I love you so much!

To my grandmother, Anna Weathington, thank you so much for your prayers. Thank you for personally taking me on my first job interview when I didn't know how to navigate through downtown Chicago. I truly thank you for always taking my calls even when you know they were going to be two hours long! You are a joy in my life and a tower of strength and I'm so blessed to be called your granddaughter!

To my auntie, Berlinda (Buffy) Hardy, thank you for always being so funny. We reminisce about our childhood so much. I still can't believe we're grown! You are the glue that holds this family together and I appreciate you for being you! Love you!

To my stepmother Alecia Knighten, thank you for always encouraging me to be independent and to live out my dreams. I may not have understood you or appreciated your advice when I was younger, but I thank you for it now! You are the best second mother a woman could ask for! Thank you for my three brothers whom I love and adore!

To my grandmother, Ruthie Smith, thank you for the special bond we have grown to share. I love you!

To my Uncles and their wives, I love each of you in my own way! You each have special gifts that make you unique but I am blessed to have each of you in my life! Love you all!

To my little brother, Max Knighten, your strength is remarkable! You have taught me to enjoy the simple things in life because it's the small things that make you the happiest! I love you!

To my youngest brother, Marcus Knighten, thank you for always encouraging me and making me laugh! I am so proud of you and I love you!

To Maia Campbell, my best friend, you have stuck by me through thick and thin since high school! Thank you for being my friend, confidante, mother of *my godchildren, my business partner, my shoulder to lean on and my right hand. You are an incredible woman and no matter what has come our way, we have always and will always get through it together! I love you and the entire Campbell-Anderson family!*

To Lois Nalls, my second best friend...I have gained a whole family because of you. You all have loved me, flaws and all, and I can't thank you enough for that! I love my Nalls Family!

To Latrisha Friend, my sister...thank you so much for the role you have played in my life! You are an amazing woman of God and I can't wait to see all the things God has in store for us! I love you all...Valerie, Lonnell and LaiLah!!!

To Asha Watson, my dearest friend and biggest cheerleader.....I can't thank you enough for believing in me and for pushing me to give birth to my books! Thank you for connecting me to my fearless mentor, Melanie Bonita, who has challenged me to get this done! I truly appreciate you both!

To Sonja and Alexis Anderson and family...you have gone above and beyond for me and I can't thank you enough for that! Thank you for believing in me and for being there every step of the way to help make my dreams come true! I can't wait until we have more fabulous adventures!

To Sheila and Michael Flemons and family...I can't thank you enough for your love and support! You both have been a tremendous blessing in my life and for that I will forever be grateful!

To Coushatta Liddell, Marilyn Johnson, Bryant Jones and Kion Willingham, my Digital Worxx Family! Thank you so much for designing my book covers, website and printed materials! You have taken my vision to levels beyond my wildest dreams! Thank you so much for all the hard work you put into making my dreams come true! You are truly talented and I love you guys very much!

To Desiree Johnson and Faces by Sadari, thank you for slaying my hair and makeup for my book cover! You ladies rock!

Burned But Not Broken

To my Editor: Tiff's Editing Café, thank you very much for services! You are appreciated!

To Pastor W.L. Rush, I, my first Pastor, thank you for teaching me to serve the Lord with the "Spirit of Excellence" and for showing me how to build the awesome relationship that I have with God today! Thank you so much Min. Kim Norwood, my sister in Christ, for your love and for introducing me to New Hope! Being a member of the New Hope Family has been a huge blessing in my life! Be blessed!

To my Illinois Media School, Chicago Vocational High School Family (IMS & CVS), Francis M. McKay and my Bryn Mawr Elementary School family, thank you all for your unwavering kindness, love, partnership and support! Erika Johnson, Ayanna Allen, Kristianna Slay, Joseph Ratliff, Mrs. Carr, Mrs. Butler, Ms. Lee, Mrs. Cox and Principal Betty Despenza-Green, I can't thank you enough for the blessings you have bestowed upon me!

To Eddie Parker, the love of my life, you are an amazing partner and companion! You have brought me so much joy and happiness and you bring out the best in me in every way. Thank you for your love and support every single day. I love you very much!

Special thank you to the firefighters, doctors, nurses and therapists that helped me during the healing and restoration process, you are appreciated!

Extra Special Thank You to Willie James for putting the fire out! I am forever grateful for the actions you took that led towards my healing process. God Bless You!

A Very Special Thank You to my family and friends, I love and appreciate you guys so much! We have been through some very difficult times together, but we are still standing! Thank you for your unconditional love! I love you all!

Table of Contents

Prologue

An innocent little girl who was still so naïve
Had no idea what kind of dreams she could possibly achieve
She had just started school, very bright I must say
Extremely lovable, the teacher's pet and a leader in her own
way
Big, beautiful brown eyes, a smile bright as the sun
When she entered into a room, you feel your day had just
begun
Her energy was captivating, she was thoughtful and smart
Her laugh was oh so adorable and she has the biggest heart
But there was another side to this astonishing little girl
The curiosity that would have killed the cat, instead shattered
her tiny innocent world
One day she came home from school, played with her younger
sister upstairs
You would think they would play simple games, like "Simon
Says" or "Musical Chairs"
But not this particular day, with curiosity at its best
She flicked a cigarette lighter, but didn't understand the flames
were too close to her chest
Her shirt caught on fire, she looked to her right for help
But her 4-year-old sister was in a state of shock, so she had to
help herself
She fled down the stairs, fire spreading, screaming and crying
for help again
When a familiar face came to her rescue with a blanket in his
hands
Then she saw her mother's face and that gave her some relief
Her skin was so hot it needed water, but they gave her
something to drink
"NO!!!" she cried, "put it here," as she pointed to her skin

Burned But Not Broken

But the fireman said "I'm sorry, you have to drink it", awww so
sad that she couldn't win

Now surrounded by doctors, nurses and some angels in
disguise

They couldn't help but do everything in their power when they
saw those weepy brown eyes

Physical therapy, months of recovery, burns healing at their
best

Leading the children to the playroom, sick and tired of all that
rest

Laughter helped her recover quickly, helping those who were in
need

Her leadership then, as it is now, constantly inspires her to
succeed

Confidence is key, her burns are healed, feeling empowered
and restored

Taking the lead in helping others fight against their self-esteem
wars

On a mission to motivate those who may not always feel pretty

We all have scars, inside or out, and are as beautiful as we can
be

Winks in the mirror, kisses are blown, wraps her arms around
her waist like wings

Saying "Hey Beautiful," I love you today," has truly boosted her
self-esteem

With affirmations igniting her love and making better choices
from within

She may be burned but she's not broken; her confidence
journey will never end!

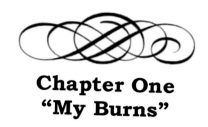

Chapter One
"My Burns"

"What is to give light must endure burning." - Viktor E. Frankl

"Help!!! Help!!!! Help me!!!!!" Screamed the six-year old girl who was on fire. "Somebody please help me!!!!" She said as she ran hysterically down the stairs to the main floor of the house. She's crying and screaming, crying and screaming when finally Willie James came out of the room and saw her on fire! "Oh my God!" He screams as he races to get the nearest blanket to put the fire out. She's crying and sobbing, "It's going to be ok, you're going to be ok," he says to her as he wrapped her up and laid her down on the sofa in the living room. He called 911 and the Chicago Fire Department rushed to 74th near Western to rescue her. It would be a day I would remember forever.

When I look back over my life and think about where God has brought me from, tears roll down my eyes every time. I realize I should have been dead at age six,

11

but there's a reason I'm still here. This was one incident that could have taken me to my grave at an early age, but only God's mercy kept me here to tell my story.

My name is Tamara but I am affectionately known to most as "Tam". My mother said I was the most loving little girl in the world and everyone always wanted me to go home with them. The problem was, I always want to follow. Even strangers on the street would see me with my mother and would shower me with compliments saying how cute and adorable I was and asked if I wanted to go with them and I would say yes. My mother said she knew then she had to keep a close eye on me because she was afraid someone would take me one day. Now that I think about it, it was because I enjoyed the attention and thought the world was full of happiness and love...that is...until bad things started happening to me. When something bad happens to you, your innocence is shattered and you never look at the world the same again.

Surely, you are wondering, how did the fire start and what was this six-year-old girl doing on fire? Well, I must admit, as a child, though loving and adorable as I could be, I was also quite mischievous. I don't know why, I just was. My mom worked second shift so she needed someone to look after my sister, Toni and I while she worked. As a result, we stayed with our babysitter, Ms.

Williams, during the week and went home on the weekends. Even though Ms. Williams had a pretty big house, upstairs, downstairs and a basement with a big backyard, it wasn't exactly a place filled with love and happiness in my eyes. There were a lot of grown folks living there and they were doing everything under the sun...smoking, drinking, partying and all kinds of craziness going on. As a child I just honestly hated being there, but my mom had to work so I didn't have a choice.

This day when I got home from school, I was playing with my then four-year-old sister in the family room upstairs. We were originally watching cartoons, but then we saw a cigarette lighter lying on the table and we began playing with it. Since everyone around us smoked, we had a pretty good idea of how this worked.

So, my sister and I were taking turns flicking the lighter. She would flick it, we'd see the fire come out, then we'd let it go and she passed it to me. I would then take the lighter and flick it until we saw the fire, then let it go. We did this for a few minutes but honestly it was getting kind of boring, however, we didn't stop. I passed it back to my sister, she had her turn and then it was my turn again. However, this time, I held the cigarette lighter a little too close to my shirt and suddenly I was engulfed in flames! My shirt was on fire while I was still in it!!! I didn't know how to put it out, so I yelled out to my sister, "Toni, go get help!" but my little sister was frozen solid. I screamed again "Toni, go get help!!!" Again, she stood there in shock. As I stood there on fire burning, I'm screaming "Toni, please go get help! Somebody help me!!!" but she couldn't move.

I had never heard the phrase "stop, drop and roll" if you're ever on fire, so I didn't know to do that. However, at that moment, I was standing near the closet by the door leading down the stairs and as the fire began spreading towards my right arm, I remember looking to the left and saw that opening. When I saw that my sister couldn't move, I took off running down the stairs, but at that point, the fire began spreading to my back and now my upper body is on fire! When I finally made it down the flight of stairs, that's when I began screaming for help again until Willie James, Ms. Williams' son, saw the fire and put it out. He rescued me from that fire and I will be forever grateful for that moment. It is the only memory I had in that house that gives me a sense of peace and gratitude. I know if he wasn't there, it is possible I would not be alive today.

Willie James called 911 and I remember the very moment when the firefighter came into the house and saw me lying on the sofa. They arrived the same time my mother did and I was in shock! I remember thinking 'wow, my mother got here quickly' because I know for a fact that she was at work. So how did she get there so quickly? I guess when your children are in trouble, you do whatever it takes to get to them as quickly as possible.

Honestly, I was so happy and relieved to see my mother that I felt a sense of peace come over me and I knew then I was going to make it through this. It's something about seeing your mother's face that gives you comfort and happiness even when you're in so much pain. I remember the firefighter approaching me and I said to him as I'm pointing to myself, "It's hot, I need water." However, he handed me a glass of water, but that's not what I wanted.

My body was hot and I needed him to pour the water all over me so that I could cool off, but that's not what he did. In my six-year-old mind, I thought that when something was on fire, you use water to cool it off, but I guess that's not the case, so I had a bit of an attitude when he didn't pour the water on my body to cool it down. He did however, put me on a gurney, put me in the ambulance and took me to Cook County Hospital, where I would spend the next three months recuperating.

Chapter Two
"My Scars"

"I think scars are like battle wounds - beautiful, in a way. They show what you've been through and how strong you are for coming out of it." - Demi Lovato

Three months was a long time to recuperate in a hospital. However, I had some really good times while I was there. When I arrived at the hospital, I was being treated for third-degree burns, which resulted in my needing a skin graft. A skin graft is when a layer of skin is surgically removed from one area of the body to another. Because my burns were spread across my upper body, my right arm and my back, the doctors had to use the skin from both of my legs to cover my third-degree burns. Therefore, my body was wrapped in a cast, both my upper body and both of my legs, which resulted in me being in a wheelchair during the recovery process. Not only did this burn leave a physical scar, but also mental and emotional scars as well.

Burned But Not Broken

Recovery was difficult at times. I remember constantly itching all the time and couldn't scratch because my body was wrapped in a cast. Don't you hate having an itch that you can't scratch? It was a difficult time because I was itching all the time. I'm sure I drove the nurses crazy during my stay because I called them all the time. They would come in and soothe me and then give me Jello or juice to make me smile.

I was in the children's ward, so the nurses were great to me, making sure I had everything I needed. My mom was there all the time but I missed hanging out with my sister. As much as I loved not being in that house, I hated that she was there without me. I was always protective of her and even though I was going through so much, I wanted to make sure she didn't suffer like I did. The one thing I knew for sure about my sister is that she was very tenacious and very mean so I knew in my heart that she was going to be fine and nobody was going to bother her. However, the separation was extremely hard on me. I was bored and lonely when visiting hours were over. Even though I made friends at the hospital with all the doctors, nurses, and other children, I still felt alone.

I couldn't see my body because I was wrapped like a tiny little mummy. The nurses had to change my bandages regularly so I was always in pain. I hated that

17

process especially when the burns were so fresh. I felt like this process was going to take forever to heal. My right arm was in a cast so I had to learn to write with my left hand. That was very awkward and it took me some time to learn because I'm right-handed and now I couldn't use my right hand to do anything. All I remember thinking is, *what a terrible choice I made the day of the fire.*

Even though I always felt the guilt, I tried to stay in good spirits. I remember one day when my mom was leaving, once she visited with me, she would always say something fun like, "see you later alligator," and I would say "after while crocodile," and one of my friends would say, "too soon baboon", as we laughed and giggled. Those were the moments I held on to that got me through the night. I'm learning more and more every day that it's the little things that go a long way.

Chapter Three
"My Pain"

"When adversity strikes, that's when you have to be the most calm. Take a step back, stay strong, stay grounded and press on." - LL Cool J

Pain, Pain, PAIN!!! I had pain coming from every angle of my body! Can you imagine being six-years-old with your body covered with fresh burns and a fresh skin graft? It is the worst pain ever! What exactly did I do to myself? How did I get here? I know for sure that if I had known how much pain I was going to be in, I WOULD NOT have been playing with a cigarette lighter! One of my favorite sayings is, "you can choose your sins, but you can't choose your consequences." – Unknown. What a price to pay for "<u>playing</u>" with a cigarette lighter!

Every single day in the hospital, the routine was the same. First, you never get any sleep because the nurses come in all hours of the night to draw your blood and take your vitals or to give you your medication so you're always tired. Then, morning would come and it's time for breakfast. Just after breakfast, it was time to change my dressings and bandages. The nurses must first remove the protective jacket that covered my bandages. I remember the jacket feeling like Velcro.

They used the jacket for various reasons. Lord knows I was a curious child. I found out that it was used to keep me from seeing what was happening underneath my bandages. Believe me if I had a chance to peek at something, I was peeking! It was also used so that the sheets and gowns wouldn't agitate my burns. Once they removed the jacket, they cut the bandages off me then removed the dressing. That's the part I absolutely hated the most!!!!

No matter how many times I went through this routine, I absolutely hated when the nurse removed my dressings! When the wounds were fresh during the healing process, the dressing would always stick to my open wounds and hurt when the dressing would be removed. It is the first layer that goes on and the last to be removed. It felt like I was on fire all over again. OMG WHAT PAIN!!!! OUCHHHHH!!!! I could cry right now just thinking about it! I hated this process. I didn't make things any better because I was pouting, kicking and screaming every single day!

Burned But Not Broken

After the nurse removed the old dressing (and after I gave her major attitude), she replaced it with a fresh one. "Ahhhh!" now this is the part I loved. The new dressing was wet and cold and it felt so good covering my open wounds. She was so good at laying them over me one by one and I felt instant relief. "Yesssss!!!!" is what I felt when the new dressing was being laid over my body. Then she wrapped me with bandages and put my outer jacket back on. That was my routine for the next three months. I was not a happy camper.

In addition to being wrapped like a mummy every day, I also had to attend physical therapy a few times a week. Since my right arm was burned and the skin was very tight, I had to learn how to use it again. I went to therapy and they made me stretch my arm as far as I could so that I could regain the use of my right arm. Let me tell you....it was an excruciating process. Who knew I was going to have to go through all of this just so I can be "normal" again?

After my 3-month stint at the hospital, the doctor finally released me to go home. Apparently, I was healing well and was able to be released. I was happy that I would get to see my sister again but was sad that we had to still live at the babysitter's house. I would have rather stayed in the hospital.

Living there was a nightmare for me. When it was time for Ms. Williams to change my dressings, she would first let me soak in the tub so that the dressings would be easy to remove. However, when the dressing didn't come off on its own, she would snatch them off my body and I would start bleeding! I remember screaming at the top of my lungs OUCHHHHHHH!!!!!!!! Then I started crying. I absolutely hated this process because it made me so sad and angry because it hurt so badly. I thought this would never end, but after some time and by the grace of God, my wounds finally healed and I didn't have to be tortured by the babysitter anymore.

Chapter Four
"My Mother's Love"
By Sharon Rosario

"You see, at the end of the day, my most important title is still 'mom-in-chief.' My daughters are still the heart of my heart and the center of my world." -Michelle Obama

"Sharon Rosario will you please come to the office?" said the voice on the steel mill plant intercom. As I heard my name called I thought to myself, *what have I done now?* When I arrived at the office my foreman told me to have a seat. He said, "I am going to tell you something and I do not want you to panic." That was a dumb thing to say because just hearing the phrase "don't panic" puts me in a panic state automatically but I said, "OK." (I thought I was going to get fired or reprimanded for something). Little did I know that would be a day I would always remember my entire life.

My boss calmly said, "I don't want you to panic because you will need all your senses to drive home

23

because your babysitter called and said your daughter has been burned." I don't believe I heard anything else he said or even if he said anything else because I was already running through the steel mill at full force towards the parking lot. I didn't wait to get permission to leave or never gave a thought to punching out on the time clock. My heart was pounding so hard I thought it would explode and my head was throbbing from all the terrible things that were running through my mind. Imagination can play some horrible tricks on the mind.

By the time I reached my car, I had to tell myself to calm down. I sat in the car trying to catch my breath with tears rolling down my cheeks. I sobbed so hard and rocked back and forth crying and moaning the words, "God not my babies, not my babies!" over and over. Then I started talking to myself saying, *OK, stop it you need to pull yourself together because you need to get there in one piece.* It took a little while for this to sink in but finally I was in good enough shape to drive. As I drove, my mantra was 'hold it together, hold it together' all the way to the babysitter's house. I don't know how I got there so fast without the police stopping me. When I pulled up and saw that the whole house was not on fire and there were no fire trucks present, I was able to let out a long slow breath.

Releasing that slow breath enabled me to find the courage to get out of the car and walk calmly into the house but it did nothing to stop the overwhelming pain I felt in my heart when I saw my baby girl, Tamara, (Tam for short) lying on the couch wrapped in wet sheets. I thought I would die when she looked up at me with those big sad, tear filled eyes and said, "Mama I'm so hot." Now, I have always believed there was a God and at that moment my belief was fortified when I quickly said a silent prayer and asked him to give me the strength not to go ballistic on everyone in that house (because all I saw was their blood on my hands) and not to break down into a blithering idiot for the sake of my child (I did not want to frighten her any more than she already was). For an instant, I just wanted to take her in my arms and run away as fast as I could to get her somewhere safe from all harm. When I snapped back to reality I demanded to know where my other daughter was and demanded that somebody tell me what the hell had happened.

Everyone started talking at once and as I was trying to listen to everyone at once but I felt my baby touch my hand and heard her softly say, "It was my fault." For a moment, I think my heart stopped because my 6-year-old baby was taking the blame for being burned. I screamed for everyone to shut the hell up and turned to my baby and asked if she could tell me what had happened. On our way to the hospital she said she could. It felt like forever getting to the hospital and once we arrived it seemed the nightmare would never end for either of us. Once we got to the hospital (the burn unit at Cook County) they took Tam into one of the emergency rooms. I was told that I had to wait outside because she had been severely burned and that the police and the Department of Child and Family Services would want to talk to me. Suddenly I heard her screaming "MOMMY!" I am not quite sure what I said or did when they would not let me go to my child; I can only remember being escorted to a chair by two security guards and we were all out of breath.

When the police showed up I explained to them what Tam had explained to me in the ambulance. They took down everything I said and told me I had to wait in a room until someone from child services had spoken with me. I asked why I needed to talk to them and they told me because any time a child is hurt for whatever reason a police report needs to be made and child protective services had to be called in to talk with the parent(s).

There must have been someone from child services on staff at the hospital because they came right in as the police walked out. The first thing the woman from child services said to me was "Do you know that we can take your children from you because of this incident? I was already in fighting mode when I jumped up from my chair, fist balled up and ready to attack when I told her, "you better call the police back in because I will kill anyone that tries to take my children." She told me to calm down and tell her what happened, which I did.

It seemed that my heart was not done being ripped apart. The doctor said that Tam had third degree burns over 75% of her upper body and that she would need blood donations, skin grafts, and cosmetic surgery. The doctors also reported that she may never be able to use her right arm much and that she would never grow breast on the right side of her body. I was just happy that she was alive and doing better, so I told them I would do whatever was needed for her. Yet again, more shredding of my heart was to come when the doctors told me that I could help with everything but unfortunately the skin grafts had to come from my baby's own body. There are simply no words I can find to tell you what was going on in my head at that time because simply using the word devastation would not suffice. Again, and again my poor baby had to go through so much to be so little.

Tamara, my little trooper, was the belle of the hospital and was loved by everyone who met her. She happily bounced back from everything they threw at her and was the support and encouragement of all the other burn victims in her ward. I brought her sister, Antoinette, (Toni for short) to visit because she was worried that her big sister was never coming home again. She had to see for herself that her sister was doing fine and this relieved her worries. I overheard Tam telling Toni "It's ok...you didn't do this, I did." and then she hugged her and patted her on the back. Up until then I did not know that Toni, only four-years-old at the time, was blaming herself for Tam getting burned. I tried to talk to Toni on the ride home about what I had overheard and she told me, "It's ok Mama, Tam said it was not my fault and for me not to be sad" and with that knowledge she was fine and never mentioned it again. One thing that I learned from my children is that whatever life throws at you, bounce back from it. I spent so much time coming and going to the hospital that I should have just rented a room there. I used to fall asleep in the chair while Tam watched TV just to get in a few hours of quality time.

Bills still had to be paid and I could not afford to lose my job so I sacrificed sleep to spend as much time with Tam at the hospital before I had to go to work. One day when I went to visit, Tam was not in her room so I thought she had gone for a test or therapy. When I asked the nurse where she was the nurse smiled at me and she said, "You have a great daughter; she takes all the children with her down the hall to the play room so they don't have to stay in their rooms all day alone; you are the only parent that visits every day." Finally, my heart was hurting for a good reason...a mother's pride in their child. I went to the play room to see Tam and after she hugged and kissed me she said, "Mom, you don't have to come every day because I know you need some rest and you need to spend more time with Toni because she doesn't get to see you as much as I do. Besides, they are taking good care of me here and I am the nurses' helper." Can you imagine taking the advice of a 6-year-old? I could not, but I did because she was right. ("Out of the mouth of babes").

I cannot tell you how many nights I cried myself to sleep once Tam got out of the hospital, especially whenever I changed the bandages on her burns or when I had to take her back to the hospital for therapy. Even today, I sometimes look at her and think back briefly to those moments but I do not dwell on them. First, they are very painful memories and I do not want her to see me sad. Secondly, I look at her today and my heart swells with pride because of how far she has come, thinking about how many times my little trooper proved those doctors wrong. Man has no idea about the awesome power of God. -Sharon Rosario

Chapter Five
"My Appearance"

"A healthy outside starts from the inside." - Robert Urich

After being burned and evaluating my scars, various thoughts would go through my mind daily. Three months had passed and it was finally time for me to go home. Honestly, I had mixed emotions about going home. I had grown to love all my doctors, nurses and other burn victims during my stay at the hospital. However, the best thing about coming home from the hospital was being reunited with my sister.

I missed her so much and because of all the emotions my sister and I had, as well as the guilt we felt that led to my hospitalization, my mother limited her visits to the hospital. I would always send word that it was not her fault, but of course, she felt some type of way. We were both very young and didn't know how to process the consequences of our actions. All of that wouldn't matter anymore because it was time for me to go home where I could be with her every day again and I couldn't have been happier. She brought me so much joy. She was my ace, my sister, my friend. We were always "thick as thieves" and everyone knew us as "Tam and Toni" everywhere we went.

I was released from the hospital and was greeted with so much love but also so much pain. I was praying that I would not have to return to Ms. Williams' house but I did. That made me sad. The only thing that made me happy was seeing my sister. She was the most beautiful dark-skinned little girl with long black hair and a pearly white smile. She's also half Puerto Rican and extremely feisty so you didn't want to mess with her. She didn't pull any punches, not even at a young age. She was my little sister and nothing could separate our sisterly love.

Now that I'm home, there were so many questions going through my mind. What would I look like now? What will people think? What will they say about me? Talk about being insecure to the 10th power! The truth is, I have always been an "overthinker" and I have always over-analyzed every situation very carefully. My thoughts were always magnified beyond reality. I can't help it...as Lady Gaga says "I was born this way." However, I was not born with patience. My six-year-old mind was running a mile a minute. When can I go home? Though I had the brightest smile, the heartiest laugh, the biggest heart and was a fearless leader at age six, I also had the biggest insecurities.

I had to deal with what I would look like physically from this day forward. I am truly blessed that the burn did not touch my face, but from the chest down. I had to face myself in the mirror every day. I now lived with third-degree burns covering a portion of my chest including my right breast, my right arm, my back and having skin grafts on both of my legs. Wow! What a major transformation for a six-year-old! This became my new reality! *How do I deal with this?* was the first of many questions that ran through my head. *How do I explain this to people? What will they think of me when I go back to school? What about my friends and teachers? How will they look at me now? What will they say?*

Have you ever felt like this before? Well, I did when the burn was still new to me. It was a difficult adjustment that I would have to get used to. Why? That's what we do in life....we adjust to the circumstances we have no control over. So how did I adjust to this new life?

Well, first, I didn't know how to adjust, but having the love from my family was a great start. They always made me feel "normal" even though I looked differently now. I remember going back to school, which of course by now I was in the first grade and everything felt strange. I felt like everybody was staring at me and I was fully dressed covering everything. That's what we do right? We hide when we feel ashamed. It reminds me of the story from the bible in Genesis where Adam and Eve were hiding from God and ran to sew figs and put them around themselves to hide their nakedness, *"and God said to them, why are you hiding? They said because we were naked. God said, who told you that you were naked? Then Adam began blaming Eve and Eve blamed the serpent for biting that apple from the Tree of Knowledge."* (Genesis 3 - Amplified Version) I understood exactly how they felt at that moment.

When people are ashamed of their looks, feelings or actions, their first thought is to find a way to hide the truth and then begin to blame others, right? Well, even though I was fully dressed, I still felt the need to hide, but honestly, there was nowhere to go. I loved school (Yes, I was a bit of a nerd and teacher's pet – don't judge me) and I would do anything that would get me out of that "house of hell" as I referred to it in my head.

Doubt, fear, and low self-esteem followed me to school and back home on a regular basis because no matter how much love I received, deep down inside, I did not believe it. I would put on the most believable smile I had and pretend that I was ok. Have you ever put on a fake smile just so that people would leave you alone? I know I did but sometimes I wanted to just yell the words "JUST LEAVE ME ALONE!!!" but you can't always do that when you're a child.

I learned years ago that your appearance is not always what you look like on the outside, but what you "appear" to be in the face of adversity. What does your appearance look like? Are you happy with how you look? Most of the time, I was not happy. I let fear and doubt dictate my wardrobe, my hairstyle and my attitude. That is not a good look. I always wanted to look confident, but when you don't feel it, you don't look it. I never wore shorts, tank tops or anything that showed my right arm or my legs. I wore slacks, jeans, and long sleeves all the time no matter how hot it was outside.

I refused to wear anything that would bring attention to my scars. I didn't want anyone asking me the usual questions, "What happened to you? How did you get burned? Does it hurt?" Having to answer any of those questions at any given time made me feel even more ashamed. All I wanted to do was crawl into a hole and die. I used to ask myself "why are people so nosey? Why are they all in my business?" Well, I knew that you couldn't say that to adults because of course you would get in trouble. However, I found that rolling my eyes became my signature move whenever I didn't want to answer any questions.

Between the ages of 6 and 14, my confidence and self-esteem were basically non-existent. No matter how cute my clothes were or how nice my hair was, I could not find my confidence. My mother could have dressed me like a nun and I wouldn't care if all of my burns were covered. However, at the ripe age of 14, my world changed.

My former stepfather took my siblings and I to a Cubs game and for the first time since my burn, I felt confident enough to wear a pair of baby blue shorts. Of course, I put on a pair of white tights underneath the shorts because I wasn't that bold, but putting on that pair of shorts was the first step towards feeling self-confident. Although it was a baby step, it was a major step for me. I felt free for the first time since my burn! I was finally in a public place wearing a pair of shorts! Thank goodness I did because it was so hot that day that I was sweating bullets. I was thinking, *it's too hot for these tights,* but I wouldn't dare take them off! No one asked about my burns and I could enjoy the game with my family and had a great time. What a proud moment in my childhood. It took me eight long years, but it finally happened and I felt free!

Elementary school was a breeze for me academically. I loved my teachers and got along with a few of the students. I attended Francis M. McKay Elementary School from kindergarten through second grade. I had fun during my years at McKay. I always loved our school song "From east to west, McKay is the best". I have very fond memories of the friends I made while I was there. Having good friends always makes your school experience a lot more fun.

I transferred from McKay to Bryn Mawr Elementary School right before the start of third grade. My sister and I were no longer living with the babysitter, which was very exciting, and now we had a new baby brother, whom we affectionately called "Lil Larry". I loved having a brother. He was born exactly seven years and three weeks after my birthday and I was thrilled.

Going to a new school was exciting. I felt like my life was going in a good direction now that we moved away. I was scared at first; I did not want to explain myself and my scars to any one at this new school, but for the most part, things went smoothly. I loved my teachers and made a few friends.

I only had one real fight in third grade, because another student kept pushing me while we stood in line to use the restroom. I had no idea why she chose to pick on me, but after school I showed her she pushed the wrong girl. She had no idea how much pinned up anger I had been holding on to about my past experiences; being burned and living in the "house of hell" where I could not do anything to change my situation. Therefore, I took all my anger out on her. She came to school with a brand new outfit and her hair done and, well, let's say she went home looking totally different. I didn't fight like Laila Ali but I did go home a champion.

*A word of advice to bullies – you don't know who you are messing with when you are bullying someone. You don't know what kind of day they are having and you don't know what's going on in their mind, so I suggest you keep your hands and your comments to yourself and stop the bullying. The harm you are causing someone else could very well backfire on you. *

I didn't have any other problems after that fight. No one else bullied me, pushed me, or talked about me (at least not to my face). I made a few friends at Bryn Mawr but had one best friend, Denise, whom I had been friends with from the fifth grade through graduation. She was biracial, born half African-American and half Caucasian, so she understood what it was like to be "different". She accepted my physical scars and we stayed friends for many years. Her parents also embraced me and broadened my horizon by taking me on their family vacations to Wisconsin, a variety of restaurants and other fun places. That part of my childhood was very memorable and I appreciate all the wonderful times we had. I graduated eighth grade in the top 10 percent of my class. I was very proud of my accomplishments.

The time had come for me to enter high school and mentally, I was not prepared. I decided to go to Chicago Vocational High School (CVS) because it was close to the new home we bought on 85th & Exchange. I didn't want to go to high school at all because I knew the kids would be different and would be meaner towards me, especially because my confidence was not fully intact.

Even though I had a breakthrough with the shorts and tights combo at the Cubs game, I was not ready to face the level of cruelty brought on by teenage peers. Children can be cruel especially when they get to high school because for some reason, they think they're better than others. I swallowed my pride, said a prayer and went to school.

When the time came for gym where we had to wear a uniform, I was terrified! I made a deal with all of my gym teachers during all four years that I would wear sweat pants underneath my uniform so that I could still be in compliance while hiding my scars. The teachers agreed and as a result, I could get through high school without having to fight to defend my honor. I met four new friends and we called ourselves the "All That" group. Our group consisted of Maia, Charity, Shiona and Regina and consisted of talent, beauty and brains. I wasn't the most confident, didn't wear the name brand clothes, but being with my girls gave me confidence. I met my best male friend, Eric, who later became my high school sweetheart by sophomore year. Now, that my life was complete with great friends and a boyfriend, I was set for the duration of my high school years.

During my tenure at CVS high school, I had no sense of style. I wore my hair pulled back, blue jeans, t-shirt and gym shoes. That was my daily attire and I didn't care. However, it was senior year and it finally happened...the moment I had been waiting for finally arrived in June 1993...senior prom! That was the day my life transformed!

Burned But Not Broken

I went to the hair salon, my stepmother did my makeup, my sister helped me get ready, my fashion design teacher made my fuchsia gown with a black cuff around the shoulders (to hide my burns), my business teacher bought my accessories, my division teacher bought my prom ticket and Eric's cousin picked us up and drop off us off in a very nice car. I can't thank this team enough for making this day so special for me! Senior prom marked the day my confidence transformed!

I didn't think about my burns at all. My focus was on being beautiful and that day I felt truly beautiful! My girls were by my side looking stunning and fabulous. That was one of the best nights of my life!!!! I finally felt confident, gorgeous, amazing and breathtaking and nobody could take that away from me! No matter who won prom queen or who had the best dress, I was dressed in confidence from head to toe! From that night forward, I found a job and always made it a point to schedule a hair appointment every two weeks! I went shopping because I wanted to look like a lady and feel confident for the rest of my life.

****

When I met my former boyfriend, Sam, he had great style and great taste. He had an idea of how he wanted his woman to dress and that changed my image forever. He liked for me to wear heels with curvy jeans and cute tops that complimented my frame. The higher the heel, the harder he fell in love. When I wore long nails and high heels, he was over the top in love! It's funny but it's true. All through college he bought all my clothes, shoes, coats, jackets, everything. He also made sure my hair and nails were done. My look was complete and he made sure of it. I loved every minute of it because my confidence was always on 10. He always dressed very well and before you know it, we were head over heels for each other. We did everything together, went on dates every weekend and spent countless hours of quality time during our relationship. We were the envy of most of our friends because of the way we loved each other. That's when I realized that being in love agreed with me. It's a great look and I love it!

I thought we were going to be "Sam & Tam" forever, and even though life has moved us on, I love being loved so when you finally receive the love you have been waiting for, hold on to it as long as you can. As Mary B. Morrison says, "Soulmates Dissipate".

Chapter Six
"My Healing,
Empowerment and Restoration"

"I'm not afraid of storms, for I'm learning how to sail my ship."- Louisa May Alcott

You have no idea how much having a peace of mind means to me! I will sit at home sometimes with the TV's and the radio off just so that I can steal moments of peace. It is mandatory in my life! I realized that after dealing with so many traumatic experiences in my life that nothing else really matters more than having peace. After spending months in the hospital when I was six and spending years at a babysitter's house I didn't like, I appreciate having peace in my life now.

I cried many days and many nights when I didn't feel beautiful or worthy. I struggled with depression and PTSD (Post Traumatic Stress Disorder). My heart and my mind suffered a lot of pain because I didn't have the confidence to get me through the day at times. When Mary J. Blige released the song "My Life", I knew for sure that song was written for me. "If you looked at my life and see what I see..." were the lyrics I had to rewind repeatedly. That song was on repeat for a long time. The entire album spoke to me. I was a young adult, living in the real world and I didn't know how to cope.

Music was my saving grace. I loved Janet Jackson, Mary J. Blige and the Hip Hop Era had just begun. I watched music videos until I memorized the lyrics and the dances. That was my true escape. I needed to be healed so I turned on the Jukebox, MTV and BET where all the music videos were playing.

I also listened to all the radio. I loved Jeanne Sparrow, Davante Stone (Stone Pony), Rick Party, Mike Love/Bad Boy Radio, First Lady, Irene "Mamacita" Mojica, Carla Box, Doug Banks and Tom Joyner, Eddie and JoBo (to name a few). "Last Night A DJ Saved My Life" helped me escape depression.

I also found comfort in House Music. Maia and I loved to go dancing where they played house music. Our favorite nightclubs were "The Riviera" and "What's Poppin". After dancing all night, we would grab a bite to eat at either Harold's Chicken or a local fast food joint that sold chicken tenders and Italian Beef sandwiches. That was the life! Music and dancing was a huge part of my healing and restoration process.

Healing

When I reached adulthood, I began my quest for peace. I began praying and searching my soul for answers. I learned that God always knows what you need, when you need it and began answering my prayers for peace. One prayer was to be baptized. I had grown up in the Jehovah's Witness religion from the ages 8-13, but at age 21, I was looking for something different. I prayed hard asking God if he wanted me to return to that religion. I visited the old Kingdom Hall that I attended as a child and felt empty. I knew then, my time there was complete.

One Saturday afternoon, I was at my hair appointment and my then stylist, Bon Jour (yes...that was his real name), was talking to me about a book he was reading dealing with the battlegrounds of our mind. He was very passionate as he spoke of what he had been learning. By the end of our conversation, he invited me to go to church with him the next day and I agreed to be his guest. He attended The Living Word Christian Center, which was in Forest Park, IL.

Now, we lived on the far eastside of Chicago, so traveling all the way to Forest Park was a journey. However, we made it there and once again, I had a life-changing experience! I listened to the message delivered by Pastor Bill Winston and what a great message! However, what happened next was the experience I was waiting for and I didn't even know it! The message led souls to come down to the altar for prayer, but if we wanted to be saved and baptized, that was our opportunity! Now, I will be honest and say, I did not grow up in church so I did not have any knowledge of what being "saved" was about. However, when I was asked if I wanted to be baptized, I was all in!

That was the language I spoke and I knew in my heart that was exactly what I wanted to do. I was very shocked that I could do it at that very moment and I took full advantage of it! Now granted, Bon Jour had slayed my hair the day before, however, none of that mattered when I put on that swim cap and baptismal robe to get baptized. I looked back at Bon Jour who was waiting for me after the service and stood there with great pride as I took that walk to the baptism pool. The moment I was waiting for arrived and I was baptized! I can't describe how amazing that feeling was to be dipped in the water and to come out feeling cleansed! It is a feeling you can't forget! I can only imagine what I had been reading about all those years in the bible where people were baptized in the Jordan River. Now, I had become one of those people and I was very proud of myself for accomplishing that goal!

This was the road to my spiritual healing and it is an experience I will always cherish. My next spiritual journey and experience was found at New Hope Community Baptist Church where W.L. Rush, I, was the Pastor. I was working at a bank and it was by the grace of God that our receptionist at the time, Kim Norwood (then Harris), who is now my sister, my friend and birthday twin, always spoke highly of her pastor and church. They had just installed a new pastor and Kim was very excited about the new direction their church was headed.

I told Kim I wanted to visit her church and one Sunday I did. It was the Sunday where they were the guest church at the Black Expo in the McCormick Place and Albertina Walker was the special guest! I was in shock! Because I did not grow up in church, I was under the impression that all Pastors had to be over 60 and that the congregation had to dress up and wear suits. I was unaware of the "come as you are" policy. I was dressed in a full two-piece white skirt suit, while everyone else, including the pastor, was dressed nice but comfortably. That was the first and the last time I wore that suit to church! I loved being free in the Lord and I loved learning about God. Thank you, Kim, for leading the way!

Being at New Hope was my first experience of being an active member in a church. I was a "Babe in Christ", meaning I was brand new to Christianity and began taking classes to learn more about the church's principles and being a servant of God. Their motto was "Serving God by Helping Others" and I knew this was where I belonged. I knew that was the calling on my life, I just did not know what it was.

I was at the right place at the right time because Pastor Rush has a gift of helping "Babes in Christ" to build a relationship with God. That's exactly what he helped me to do. He challenged me to start praying five minutes a day and then taking the time to listen to what God had to say in return.

Completing that challenge daily made me fall in love with God. I began talking to God about everything in my life. I prayed for everything, no matter how big or how small. I just fell in love with the idea that I could talk to God always. My favorite part of the service at church was altar call. I loved how I could lay on the altar and give my problems to the Lord. I felt free!

Now that I had been blessed with a great church home and a new church family, I began to commit myself to church as much as possible. Whenever the doors were opened, I was there. I had a thirst for knowledge and to see what God had to say to me. Have you ever had a hunger and thirst for God that you just couldn't get enough? Have you ever longed to get to that quiet place where you could talk to God about your day?

That was me, then and now. I LOVE the relationship I have built with God and I appreciate the foundation that was laid to help me get there. It provided me with a spiritual healing that my soul cried out for. My soul needed to be healed and I found healing in prayer. I was on a quest for healing and peace and slowly but surely, I received it. Matthew 7:7-8 says, "7) Ask, and it will be given to you; seek, and you will find; knock, and it will be opened to you. 8) For everyone who asks receives, and he who seeks finds, and to him who knocks it will be opened." (New International Version)

I could have easily turned to drugs and alcohol based on the physical scars and emotional pain I was in, but instead, I chose to turn to God to let him heal my pain. I had finally found the healing for my soul.

Empowerment

One of the synonyms for empowerment is permission. I like that synonym because I realized I gave myself permission to be beautiful, to be healed, to be empowered and to be restored to my rightful position. I didn't know what I was supposed to do in life, but I always knew I was a leader with an entrepreneurial spirit. I knew that because every business I had in the past always allowed me to work independently and was geared towards me being my own boss, so I knew I would own my own business someday.

I had been selling products since I was in my early 20's, but it just didn't seem to be the right fit. I couldn't seem to sell makeup, body butters, or insurance but I knew one day I would find my niche and I did. Writing and speaking became my passion. When I gave my first speech in college, I knew I was born for this. When I wrote my first poem, several other poems followed. I met someone who had drive, dedication and determination and that drove me to writing books.

My dream was to write a children's book that would encourage children with scars. I wanted them to know that they are still beautiful no matter what scars they lived with. That dream came true for me when I published and released "Kaiyla B. – That's Me – Dashing and Confident" in 2013. Since I was not confident after I had been burned, it is my passion to empower children to feel confident about themselves at an early age.

Shortly thereafter, I began writing my own memoirs, this book, "Burned But Not Broken". It was the hardest thing I ever had to do. I relived every word, cried excessively, forgave myself, healed, empowered and restored my confidence so that I could be a testimony to someone in need.

Restoration

Even though I have gone through the excruciating pain of being burned, and the physical, emotional and spiritual process of being healed, there was a purpose for my pain. Do you think I honestly would have burned myself if I had known the journey ahead of me? Of course not! However, I have come to understand my purpose. I needed to tell others about my healing. I needed to share with others the painful process of being burned, the scars, the emotional and physical insecurities so that I can help bring restoration to someone who feels broken. I didn't know I was chosen to be a vessel for the people who battled with the images they see in the mirror every day.

Even though I absolutely detested the pain and the process, I understood my purpose and I have made the choice to fulfill that purpose to the best of my abilities. I had no idea that when I wore a tank top or a skirt that it would boost the confidence of someone else who may be struggling with insecurities. I have devoted my time to making a positive difference by increasing a person's confidence one day at a time.

I want people to be restored mentally, emotionally, physically and spiritually just like I was. It's a great feeling to now look at myself in my mirror with a renewed confidence and a new love for myself knowing that I am finally living with a purpose and making a difference in the world. Yes, I have endured hurtful comments and judging eyes, but I was also doing it to myself. Now having the courage, I set myself free from that burden. I forgave them and I forgave myself. Now when I look in the mirror, I say, **"HEY BEAUTIFUL! <u>YOU MAY BE BURNED, BUT YOU'RE NOT BROKEN</u>!"**

Chapter Seven
"My Confidence"

"Turn your wounds into wisdom." – Oprah Winfrey

One lesson I have learned in life is that "beauty is only skin deep". When you can look past your physical, emotional and mental scars and love yourself unconditionally, it is one of the greatest feelings in the world! That's real love. When others can love you unconditionally, despite your scars, your appearance, your past and your pain, that is a bonus! In the words of one of the world's greatest voices of all time, Whitney Houston, "Learning to yourself...it is the greatest love of all!" (Greatest Love of All)

Today, I wear my scars as a badge of honor. Years ago, my dad asked me if I wanted to get cosmetic surgery to cover my scars and my response was, "No Daddy...if I cover my scars, no one will ever believe that I was burned and I won't be able to help anyone else who has scars."

The look of pride filled his eyes that day. He realized that I understood my purpose in life and that made him extremely proud of his one and only daughter.

There are three lessons that I have learned on this journey towards my confidence:

Love Myself – As William Shakespeare said, "To thine own self be true." I live by this quote because my truth is, *I am burned, but I am not broken.* I have learned my purpose in life and have seized the opportunity to share my story to help others overcome their shame, guilt and fear. Don't let anyone put you inside of a box and don't let fear force you inside that box. King David said in Psalm 139:14 "I praise you because I am fearfully and wonderfully made; your works are wonderful, I know that full well." *New International Version (NIV).*

I live for the summertime where I can flaunt my tank tops, shorts, mini-skirts and swimwear. One day I walked into an insurance office wearing a strapless jumpsuit and one of the agents said to me, "You just blessed me." All I did was walk in the door! I sat there for almost an hour discussing insurance options before she shared with me why I blessed her. She finally shared her story and said, "I was burned when I was a child and I never show my scars to anyone except my family and my boyfriend." I could tell this lady was a little older than I was and without me saying a word, I walked into her office and blessed her. My original purpose was to walk in and purchase insurance but God's purpose was to set this woman free from fear, guilt and shame! I knew at that moment that I was being used by God to restore confidence in the lives of others.

Fear Not – One of my favorite scriptures is Isaiah 41:10, "Fear not, for I am with you; Be not dismayed, for I am your God. I will strengthen you, Yes, I will help you, I will uphold you with my righteous right hand." New King James Version (NKJV). The acronym for F.E.A.R. is "False Evidence Appearing Real". When you remove the "false evidence" that is keeping you from achieving your confidence, you will conquer your fears!

There were many days in my childhood where I feared what people would say or think about me. As I got older, I realized that people will talk about you no matter who you are. You could be rich or poor, extraordinary or average, people will find a reason to talk about you. That means that they are insecure and they are in pain, which is why they feel the need to talk about you. I have been healed, delivered and set free from shame, guilt and fear, and now walk in faith and confidence.

Dust Off The Ashes And Forgive Yourself – Bruce Lee said, "Mistakes are always forgivable, if one has the courage to admit them." Have the courage to acknowledge your mistakes and forgive yourself for making them. We are not perfect, so there is no reason to keep beating yourself up over the mistakes that you have made. My mother told me that on the day I was burned, she was so angry at the babysitter and her son for leaving us unattended, and right at that moment when she was about to unleash her anger towards him, I reached out my hand to her, during all my pain and said, "Mom, it's not his fault, it was mine."

Even at a young age, I acknowledged my mistakes. It took years for me to forgive myself and let go of the guilt and shame, but when I finally did. I finally felt free! It took me years to learn that lesson, but today, I have learned to forgive myself every day for the mistakes I have made. Due to the mistakes I made in the past, I found myself being a perfectionist. I wanted to do everything right to please everyone around me. I found out later in life that you cannot live your life to please other people. People will never appreciate your sacrifice! Live your life to please God and to please yourself! Take the time to find out what makes you happy, what makes you feel good and what makes you complete. Make decisions that will bring you peace, not harm. These are the blessings that will give you true happiness at the end of the day! My favorite scripture in the bible is Jeremiah 29:11, "For I know the plans I have for you," declares the Lord, "plans to prosper you and not to harm you, plans to give you hope and a future." New International Version (NIV)

Thank you for joining me through this journey that inspired my confidence. I hope you learned from my mistakes and remember, "Don't play with fire because you will get burned." If you are ever on fire, please "Stop, drop and roll". God knew you would go through the things that you are going through in life, but he also sends people to cross your path to help you conquer your battles! I appreciate all the love I have received throughout my life, but more importantly, I am thankful that I have found the courage to love myself and to live a life full of love, laughter and passion!

I Am H.E.R. – Healed.Empowered.Restored!

The End!

Affirmations

Saying these affirmations daily can help you on your journey towards self-confidence.

- ➤ *I will love myself with all my heart.*

- ➤ *I will forgive myself every day.*

- ➤ *I will let go of fear, guilt and shame.*

- ➤ *I was created to be confident.*

- ➤ *I am healed, empowered and restored.*

Now wrap your arms around yourself and blow yourself a kiss!

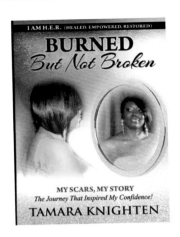

ABOUT THE AUTHOR

Tamara Knighten is a woman inspired by her own journey to feel special. Affectionately known as "Tam", she was burned at age six and has been on a mission to inspire people to feel special no matter what their circumstances are. She is extremely passionate about building self-confidence in the lives of young people and inspiring them to become productive citizens. She is fun, fierce and fabulous and wants every person to feel special. She writes poetry and books, and has designed motivational workshops to inspire, empower and enhance the lives of adults and children.

Tamara Knighten lives in Chicago, Illinois.

You can visit her at www.tamaraknighten.com.

49337552R00035

Made in the USA
Middletown, DE
13 October 2017